ALL-STAR SPORTS PUZZLES

SOCCER

GAMES, TRIVIA, QUIZZES AND MORE!

Jesse Ross

RAINCOAST BOOKS
www.raincoast.com

Raincoast Books gratefully acknowledges the financial support of the Province of British Columbia through the BC Arts Council and the Book Publishing Tax Credit and the Government of Canada through the Canada Council for the Arts and the Book Publishing Industry Development Program (BPIDP).

Edited by Brian Scrivener
Interior design by Warren Clark
Typesetting and additional design by Five Seventeen

Library and Archives Canada Cataloguing in Publication

Ross, Jesse, 1986–
    Soccer / Jesse Ross.

(All-star sports puzzles)
ISBN 13: 978-1-55192-820-3
ISBN 10: 1-55192-820-5

    1. Soccer—Miscellanea.
    2. Puzzles.
    I. Title.
    II. Series: Ross, Jesse,1986– . All-star sports puzzles.

GV1493.R657 2008   796.33402   C2007-904847-1

Library of Congress Control Number: 2007933935

Raincoast Books
9050 Shaughnessy Street
Vancouver, British Columbia
Canada V6P 6E5
www.raincoast.com

In the United States:
Publishers Group West
1700 Fourth Street
Berkeley, California
94710

Raincoast Books is committed to protecting the environment and to the responsible use of natural resources. We are working with suppliers and printers to phase out our use of paper produced from ancient forests. This book is printed with vegetable-based inks on 100% ancient-forest-free, 40% post-consumer recycled, processed chlorine- and acid-free paper. For further information, visit our website at www.raincoast.com/publishing/.

Printed in Canada by Webcom

10 9 8 7 6 5 4 3 2 1

CONTENTS

Trivia

Fill Me In

Puzzles

CONTENTS

Long Puzzles

Throughout the book, you will find additional facts at
the bottom of each page, and occasionally a **Bonus question.**
These are extra-hard questions for expert soccer fans only!

Check out our website: **www.allstarsportspuzzles.com**

Note: All puzzles are accurate, to the best of our knowledge, as of October 2007.

The Great Search

The last names of 18 soccer stars are hidden below. They are written forwards or backwards, and are hidden diagonally, horizontally and vertically. Every player in the puzzle either won the FIFA World Player of the Year or the European Footballer of the Year award. After you've crossed out each name, the leftover letters spell out the name of the oldest ever World Player of the Year winner, as of 2007.

R	C	A	N	N	A	V	A	R	O
F	O	C	R	U	Y	F	F	I	N
M	V	N	A	B	I	O	G	E	O
A	O	H	A	E	W	G	W	K	V
T	N	Z	O	L	A	O	N	F	O
T	A	I	D	B	D	E	C	I	K
H	L	D	L	L	H	I	R	G	H
A	E	A	A	C	A	A	N	O	C
U	B	N	V	N	M	N	I	H	I
S	O	E	I	O	A	V	P	A	O
R	H	R	R	E	M	M	A	S	T
S	N	E	D	V	E	D	P	O	S

Names

Roberto BAGGIO
Igor BELANOV
Fabio CANNAVARO
Johan CRUYFF
Luis FIGO
Lothar MATTHAUS

Pavel NEDVED
Michael OWEN
Jean-Pierre PAPIN
RIVALDO
ROMARIO
RONALDINHO

RONALDO
Matthias SAMMER
Andriy SHEVCHENKO
Hristo STOICHKOV
George WEAH
Zinedine ZIDANE

Oldest winner: ___ ___ ___ ___ ___   ___ ___ ___ ___ ___ ___ ___ ___

Frenchman Just Fontaine holds the record for most goals in any World Cup, with an amazing 13 in 1958. Even though this was his only World Cup, as of 2008 he is third on the all-time list of most goals scored at the tournament.

Finish the Cross

Fill in the crossword grid by answering each clue, corresponding to the number in the grid.

Across

1) World Cup 2006 winner

2) Raul Gonzalez and Xabi Alonso's native country

5) Players heading the ball often do this

9) This type of kick is also a mode of transport

11) Colour in the referee's pocket

12) Type of kick

13) 20 players on the field can't use these

15) Typical colour at a soccer game

17) "Man ____!"

18) Type of shot that often fools goalies

19) Real _____

22) _____ Milan

23) Type of tackle

Pele and Uwe Seeler are the only two players who have scored in four different World Cups (both scoring in 1958, '62, '66 and '70).

Down

1) Time after the 90-minute mark

3) FIFA Fair _____

4) Throw - ____

6) Central position

7) _____ and go

8) Lots of goals are scored with this

10) _____ League

14) A forward may call "_____ me!"

15) Olympic _____

16) Many domestic team names start or end with this acronym

20) Injured players may apply this

21) _____ play (i.e., free kicks, corners)

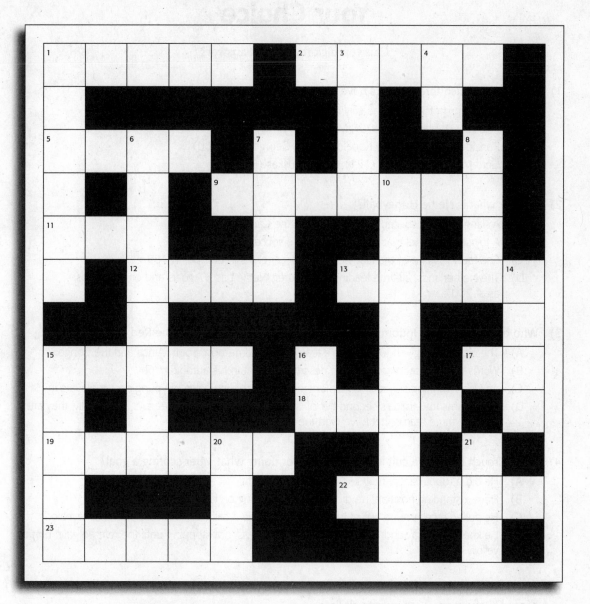

Bonus: Of the 20 teams playing in England's Premier League in 2007–08, how many can you name?

Your Choice

Can you pick the correct answer?

1) **As of 2007, which three players have scored the most goals in international play?**
   A) Mia Hamm (158), Kristine Lilly (129), Ali Daei (109)
   B) Pele (202), Maradona (175), Mia Hamm (148)
   C) Ronaldo (115), Cristiano Ronaldo (101), George Best (100)
   D) Gerd Muller (151), Pele (121), Ferenc Puskas (89)

2) **Who or what is Nettie Honeyball?**
   A) A slang term for soccer, used primarily in the Caribbean.
   B) A toy set by Mattel that includes an edible soccer ball and net.
   C) She founded one of the first women's soccer clubs in Europe, in 1894.
   D) The Netherlands' all-time leading goal scorer; Nettie has 37 goals and only 35 caps, as of 2007.

3) **Who or what are "The Indominitable Lions," "Bafana Bafana" and "The Red Devils"?**
   A) The nicknames given to the men's teams from Cameroon, South Africa and the Congo.
   B) Words Pele affectionately used to describe his feet in his autobiography.
   C) An Oscar-winning series of documentaries about the struggles of young soccer players in Haiti.
   D) Club teams in Canada's second-tier of women's soccer, the W2-League. Incidentally, they are the only three teams that have won the league title.

4) **Peter Crouch became a cult icon in England for doing what, after scoring a goal?**
   A) He did a robot dance, now known as "The Crouch."
   B) From a standing position, he did a front flip, landing on his feet.
   C) He pulled a cell phone out of his shorts and made a call (to his mother, he later revealed).
   D) He knelt to the ground and starting eating the grass, not stopping until the referee gave him a yellow card.

5) **One hundred and twelve games were played at World Cup 2006. How many goals were scored? How many were own goals?**
   A) 355 goals, 13 own goals
   B) 98 goals, 9 own goals
   C) 147 goals, 4 own goals
   D) 239 goals, 0 own goals

Brazil is the only country that has played in all 18 World Cups.

6) What do the following have in common: Love, Loco and Flavio?

A) They were the three official mascots of World Cup 2006.

B) They are all nicknames given to players on Angola's national team.

C) They are the three words Portuguese Prime Minister Jose Socrates used to describe Luis Figo, after the star retired. Socrates apparently "loved his crazy flavour."

D) They are the names of Reebok's new 2008 soccer cleats. The names were chosen by online voting.

7) Which club teams provided the most players for World Cup 2006?

A) Arsenal (15), Chelsea (15) and Milan (13)

B) Real Madrid (17), Barcelona (11) and Bayern Munich (11)

C) Al-Ittihad (14), Al-Hilal (14) and Chelsea (13)

D) Shakhtar Donetsk (16), Juventus (14) and Manchester United (12)

8) As of 2007, what is the biggest transfer fee ever paid for a player?

A) US$102,550,000, Cristiano Ronaldo (Bayern Munich to Manchester United)

B) US$59,790,000, Andriy Shevchenko (A.C. Milan to Chelsea)

C) US$73,741,000, Luis Figo (Barcelona to Real Madrid)

D) US$91,679,000, Zinedine Zidane (Juventus to Real Madrid)

9) What is the G-14?

A) The term used to describe the top 14 countries in the world, according to the FIFA rankings.

B) An organization of 18 top football clubs in Europe, formed to promote "cooperation and good relations" between the teams and FIFA.

C) A formation used by Argentina in 1990, centering on the concept of having 14 strikers (11 on the field plus three subs).

D) The producer of Winning Eleven, the bestselling soccer video game franchise in the world.

10) Why were the 1999 and 2003 FIFA Women's World Cups both held in the U.S.?

A) Because no other nations made a formal bid to host the 2003 event.

B) The 2003 World Cup was going to be held in Canada, but the main stadium collapsed four months before the tournament, and the games had to be moved south.

C) The location of the Women's World Cup is determined by the winner of the previous Cup, and the USA won in 1999.

D) The 2003 World Cup was scheduled for China but had to be moved because of the SARS epidemic.

In 1998, Romanian first-division club **Jiul Petrosani** traded midfielder Ion Radu for $2,500 worth of pork, and transferred Liviu Baicea for 10 balls and some jerseys.

Lost Letters

Fill in the missing letter in the middle to complete the last letter of the player's name on the left, and the first letter of the name on the right. After you have finished each name, the letters down the middle spell out the name of the youngest-ever World Cup player, at 17 years and 41 days old.

Gianluigi Buffo	___	wankwo Kanu
Romari	___	liver Kahn
Gerd Mulle	___	aul Gonzalez
Philip Lah	___	ichael Bradley
Gabriel Batistut	___	ndriy Shevchenko
Arjen Robbe	___	icolas Burdisso
John Care	___	ayne Rooney
Petr Cec	___	ernan Crespo
Luca Ton	___	van Zamarano
Dirk Kuy	___	hierry Henry
Pel	___	ddie Pope
Jeff Agoo	___	amuel Eto'o
Ali Dae	___	van Hurtado
Pavel Nedve	___	idier Drogba
Miroslav Klos	___	ric Wynalda

Youngest player:

_____

Bonus: In 2002, Turkey's Hakan Sukur scored the fastest goal in World Cup history. How long did it take him to score the goal?
A) 2.8 seconds; B) 11 seconds; C) 19 seconds; D) 39 seconds

Who Am I?

See if you can figure out who these clues point towards, in the fewest clues possible.

A

1) I wore number 11 until 2007, but then I switched to number 30.
2) I was traded to Real Salt Lake in late 2006, though I didn't last long there.
3) I am the youngest-ever player in MLS to both start a game and score a goal.
4) Born in 1989 in Ghana, I became one of the youngest players ever to sign a professional sports contract in the U.S., at age 14. In 2007, I joined Portugal's Benfica.

Who am I?_____

B

1) I was the youngest ever to play on a U.S. National team, at age 15.
2) I wrote a book titled *Go for the Goal: A Champion's Guide to Winning in Soccer and Life*.
3) I won four NCAA titles with the University of North Carolina, in 1989, '90, '92 and '93. In 1991, I took the year off to win my first of two World Cups.
4) I am the leading scorer in international women's soccer, with 136 goals and 114 assists.

Who am I?_____

C

1) I have scored 11 goals in my professional career.
2) I was often sighted in the other team's penalty box, and I could nearly throw the ball that far.
3) I am Denmark's most capped player, with 129 games (30 as captain).
4) In my years in the Premiership, I held the opposition scoreless 42 percent of the time, the greatest percentage in history. I was voted World's Greatest Goaltender in 1992 and 1993 while with Manchester United.

Who am I?_____

Guinness record: In 2003, Brazilian Martinho Eduardo Orige juggled a soccer ball for 19 hours and 30 minutes straight, without letting the ball touch the ground.

Through Ball

Each of these random rows of letters has a soccer-related term or name hidden within. Fill in the one missing letter in the centre to reveal the word. For example, with "FONTESOC ___ ERBASINS," add a C to the centre to reveal "Soccer."

1)   A R A S T E P O ___ E R T A N D I A

2)   L A N A M A R A ___ O N A M A N O A

3)   E N I T R E W O ___ L D C U P P L E

4)   Y O G I G O B I ___ A C K P A S S W

5)   D E N G O A L P ___ S T R E A L E D

6)   S E R A N T E N ___ A C K L E N T A

7)   L O P I T H R O ___ I N A S L E L O

8)   H O U S E T I S ___ R I K E R N A L

9)   Z O M B A T H E ___ D E R V I N G S

10) L O S H I N P A ___ S S I O N C K E

11) J A L E F R I C ___ R N E R C R E L

12) L O P E N A L T ___ L O P E N A L T

13) I L T R E D C A ___ D E N K H I A L

On April 9, 2001, Australia set the record for the largest margin of victory in an international match with a 21–0 thrashing of Tonga. Two days later, they broke the record again with a 31–0 win over American Samoa, including 13 goals by Archie Thompson. Both games were World Cup qualifiers.

Confused Clubs

Can you match these teams with the leagues they play in?

Tottenham Hotspur FC	Major League Soccer
FC Barcelona	J-League Division 1
Olympique Lyonnais	Italian Serie A
FC Bayern Munich	La Liga
AS Roma	Ligue 1
Celtic FC	Scottish Premier League
DC United	Bundesliga
Kashima Antlers	Ukrainian Premier League
Club Deportivo Guadalajara	Russian Premier League
AFC Ajax	Primera Division de Mexico
FC Spartak Moscow	English Premier League
FC Dynamo Kyiv	Primera Division Argentina
SL Benfica	Eredivisie
Club Atlético Boca Juniors	Portuguese Liga

Bonus: The second-round match between Portugal and the Netherlands at World Cup 2006 set a record for the most what?

Round and Round

This puzzle goes in a spiral, starting with the top left corner and working around until all the spaces are filled up. The start of the next clue is formed by the last one or two letters of the previous answer. The number in brackets at the end of each clue gives the number of letters in the answer. Try working backwards if you get stuck.

1) Non-competitive international match (8)

2) Card (6)

3) Worst kind of goal (3)

4) Behind goalie (3)

5) Offside _____ (4)

6) Reason for a whistle (7)

7) The penalty box is commonly defined using these units of measurement (5)

8) _____ over (4)

9) Top English league, abbreviation (3)

10) _____ Donovan (6)

11) Not offside (two words) (6)

12) Peter Schmeichel & Jon Dahl Tomasson's native country (7)

13) Jersey, shorts & socks (3)

14) "You've got _____!" (4)

15) Peter Crouch & Steven Gerrard's native country (7)

16) Players constantly do this with the ball (7)

The Transfer

						1	2
8		9		10			
14				15			
13							
7						11	3
		16					
				12			4
		6				5	

Italy, as winner of the **2006 World Cup**, received $21.5 million from FIFA. Each country that qualified received $5.9 million dollars. African qualifier Togo has an average income per person of less than $400 per year.

The Transfer

By changing only one letter at a time, can you make the top word become the bottom word?
Be careful, each letter you substitute as you go must make a new word. For example, to change
the word GAME into the word SAND, you could go: Game - Same - Sane - Sand.

1) Hand

_____

_____

Ball

2) Shoe

_____

Boot

3) Start

_____

_____

Score

4) Chip

_____

_____

Shot

5) Best

_____

Pass

6) Pele

_____

_____

Wins

7) Post

_____

_____

_____

Line

8) Foot

_____

_____

_____

Card

In 1992–93, only 11 players in the **English Premier League**
were born outside of the UK. In 2005–06, 45 percent
of the players were born elsewhere.

Hidden Players

The last names below have been hidden in the grid, starting with the central letter S and extending out. The letters can be connected on either side, above, below or diagonally. The same letter cannot be used twice in the same name. Watch out, two of the names listed below are not actually hidden in the puzzle. Can you figure out which two?

H	K	E	K	I	R	E
A	B	I	S	O	O	T
O	M	I	T	H	L	N
F	S	P	S	A	G	W
D	R	E	I	H	E	M
O	E	N	L	V	A	B
G	K	S	E	H	C	U

Names

William SAGNOL
Louis SAHA
Oswaldo SANCHEZ
Godfrey SAPULA
Clarence SEEDORF
Maxsim SHATSKIKH

Andriy SHEVCHENKO
Dean SHIELS
Thulani SHIVAMBU
Myron SHONGWE
Diyo SIBISI
Tiago SILVA

SIMAO
Gionasa SPINESI
Paul STALTERI
Anthony STOKES

Bonus: As of 2007, what is the largest transfer fee ever paid for a goalie? Which teams were involved, and who was the goalie?

What Am I?

See if you can figure out what these clues point towards, in as few clues as possible.

A

1) I was first seen in 1930.
2) I used to be the Jules Rimet, but I was stolen.
3) I now stand 14.5 inches tall and I'm made of 18 carat gold.
4) Fabio Cannavaro hoisted me in 2006 in Germany.

What am I?_____

B

1) I was first conceived in 1989 by Joao Havelange.
2) In 1991 I was only made up of 12, but since 1999 I've had 16.
3) Normally I move around, and in 2007 I was in China.
4) My 1999 final had an attendance of 90,185, more than any other women's sporting event in history.

What am I?_____

C

1) I will leave you upside down.
2) In other languages I'm known as Chilena, Fallruckzieher, Seitfallzieher and Brassespark.
3) I make Lance Armstrong proud.
4) I should only be attempted by expert players who don't mind falling on their heads.

What am I?_____

FIFA referees have a mandatory retirement age of 45.

World of Soccer

Put these countries into their proper place in the lists, corresponding to which nations have won the most World Cups, in both the men's and women's tournaments. The numbers in brackets represent the number of World Cups won, as of 2008. Cross out each country as you fill them in. Good luck!

Germany	Brazil	Italy	Uruguay
USA	England	Norway	France
	Germany	Argentina	

Men:

#1) _____ (5)

#2) _____ (4)

#3) _____ (3)

#4) _____ (2)

_____ (2)

#5) _____ (1)

_____ (1)

Women:

#1) _____ (2)

_____ (2)

#2) _____ (1)

The SuperLiga held its inaugural tournament in 2007. Modeled after the Champions League, the tournament featured eight top teams from MLS and Mexico's Primera Division. CF Pachula took home the US$1 million purse.

The Starting Lineup

The players' names below are listed according to their length. Fit them into their proper place in the grid; there is only one correct place for each word. To start off, find the only three-letter space for "Ono," and go from there. Good luck!

3 Letters
Ono

4 Letters
Cris
Ince
John
Kahn
Mora
Noor
Saha
Srna

5 Letters
Agboh
Ameen
Barry
Kalov
Lewis
Reina
Saidi
Villa

6 Letters
Convey
Howard
Magnin
Reasco
Sancho
Shilla
Ustari

7 Letters
Asamoah
Bolanos
Borhani
Bosnjak
Fonseca
Hansson
Jaliens
Maniche
Mohamed

8 Letters
Arellano
Azofeifa
Borgetti
Campbell
Heitinga
Nekounam
Sneijder

In 2007, 27-year-old Panagiotis Pontikos of **Olympos Xylofagou** (third-division Cyprus league) scored a record 16 goals in one game, vs. SEK Ayios Athanasios. He scored goals at 3, 20, 33, 35, 47, 50, 55, 56, 58, 61, 68, 75, 76, 83, 86 and 87 minutes.

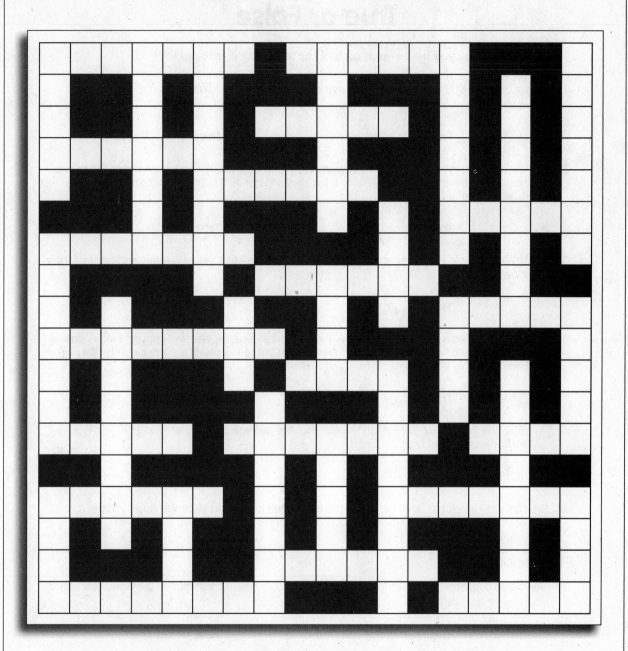

Bonus: How many of the 16 nations that qualified for the 2007 Women's World Cup can you name?

True or False

Can you figure out if each of the following is true or false?

1) Going back to 1900, the 12 greatest margins of victory in an international game, friendly or otherwise, have all happened since 1997.

True   **False**

2) For the first time ever at the 2007 FIFA Women's World Cup, money was given out to the teams. The first place team received $1 million dollars, second got $800,000, and teams exiting in the first round each received $200,000.

True   **False**

3) As of 2007, only four different managers have won the English Premier League, and none of them have been English.

True   **False**

4) In 1962, FIFA filed a lawsuit against the National Football League, claiming copyright infringement for using the word "football." The lawsuit was thrown out of the courts, on the grounds that FIFA had no ownership of the word.

True   **False**

5) In 1992, the first year of the English Premiership, the average player salary was US$149,475. In 2004, the average was US$1,347,271.

True   **False**

6) Manchester United has been playing in the top league in England since the club's inception, in 1892. They are the only Premiership club that has never been relegated (sent down).

True   **False**

7) As of 2007, Joseph "Sepp" Blatter, FIFA President, is the ninth-richest man in the world (according to *Forbes* magazine).

True   **False**

In the **1998 Swedish Championship**, winners AIK Stockholm scored fewer goals than every other team in the league – only scoring 25 times in 26 games. Talk about timely goals!

8) Pele has an asteroid named after him, "2202 Pele." It crosses the orbit of Mars, and is known as a Near-Earth asteroid. It was discovered in 1972 by Arnold Klemola.

True   **False**

9) There is a Homeless World Cup. The fifth annual event was held in Denmark in 2007. Russia won the 2006 title, which featured 48 nations and 496 players, all of whom lived on the street or made their entire income selling street newspapers.

True   **False**

10) *Mario Strikers Charged*, the Nintendo Wii soccer game, was awarded the illustrious G4 Game of the Year in 2007, thanks largely to the revolutionary motion-sensing foot controller. It was also the bestselling video game of the year, despite being released in July.

True   **False**

11) Until a FIFA ruling in 1971, it was legal to put two goalkeepers in the net at the same time.

True   **False**

12) The 2006 Czech Republic World Cup team made history. Why? Because they had four different pairs of brothers on the squad: Petr & Marek Cech, Pavel & Milan Nedved, Jaroslav & Jan Plasil, and Libor & Tomas Zapotocny.

True   **False**

13) A Guinness World Record for the longest continuous soccer game was set in 2007, when two British teams played for 30 hours and 30 minutes straight. The final score was Stratford Enterprise 138 - Exeter Fury 105, and they raised the equivalent of $16,000 for CrimeStoppers.

True   **False**

14) Frenchman Amadou Gueye bounced a soccer ball on his chest 27 consecutive times on national television.

True   **False**

15) As of 2007, no player in the English Premier League has worn a number higher than 59.

True   **False**

Real Madrid won the first five **UEFA Champions League** tournaments. They have won a record nine titles.

Spot the Fake

Below are 12 teams who played in top soccer leagues around the world in 2007, and four made-up teams. Can you spot the fake clubs?

Racing Santander	Energie Cottbus
Getafe	Empoli
Reading	Bayer Leverkusen
Figaro Figazio	Le Mans
Sampdoria	ACFCNA
Nice	Toulouse
Volley	Real Salt Lake
Chivas USA	Horkin Famplo

French club Lyon is the first team from one of Europe's big five leagues to win **six consecutive championships**, from 2001–02 to 2006–07. They also finished second in 2000–01.

Missing Leaders

The last names of the all-time leading goal scorers from 20 different nations are hidden below. They are written forwards or backwards, and are hidden diagonally, horizontally and vertically. Watch out, "Abdullah" is hidden twice. After you've crossed out each name, the leftover letters spell out the name of Spain's all-time leading goal scorer.

S	T	A	L	Y	A	N	I	B	R
A	A	N	O	T	L	R	A	H	C
K	A	U	P	V	L	T	A	A	L
S	G	R	E	E	I	O	B	N	L
U	E	N	U	S	L	D	D	E	E
P	O	N	T	I	U	E	U	S	D
B	N	U	A	L	M	Z	L	L	Y
D	T	A	L	M	U	L	L	E	R
A	N	A	A	L	U	E	A	I	U
E	H	H	S	U	R	A	H	N	K
I	O	H	A	S	S	A	N	Z	U
M	J	R	E	L	L	O	K	G	S

Names

Bashar ABDULLAH
Majed ABDULLAH
Gabriel BATISTUTA
Hristo BONEV
Bobby CHARLTON
Ali DAEI
Hossam HASSAN

Stern JOHN
Jan KOLLER
Kazuyoshi MIURA
Hussain Saeed MOHAMMED
Gerd MULLER
Poul NIELSEN
PELE

Ferenc PUSKAS
Ian RUSH
Sven RYDELL
Kiatisuk SENAMUANG
Hakan SUKUR
Adnan Al TALYANI

Spanish goal leader: ___ __ __ __ __ __ __ __ __ __ __ __ __

Bonus: Can you name the nationalities of the 20 players above?

Hidden Countries

Ten countries are hidden below, starting with the central letter S and extending out. The letters can be connected on either side, above, below or diagonally. The same letter cannot be used twice in the same name. All countries have played in the World Cup at least once. How many can you find?

A	R	B	A	B	L	A
I	A	N	I	L	R	G
L	D	U	A	E	N	E
K	T	O	S	P	Z	D
H	O	C	L	W	E	T
A	E	R	O	V	I	N
F	R	I	C	A	T	Z

Bonus: Which countries have been in the last five World Cup finals, going back to 1990 in Italy? What were the final scores?

Back to Basics

Can you tell if the words below refer to a player on the Brazilian national team, a country on the FIFA rankings or a word for soccer in a different language? Circle the correct choice.

1) Djibouti

Player   Country   Word

7) Sao Tome e Principe

Player   Country   Word

2) Calcio

Player   Country   Word

8) Naldo

Player   Country   Word

3) Josue

Player   Country   Word

9) Nogomet

Player   Country   Word

4) Vanuatu

Player   Country   Word

10) Vagner Love

Player   Country   Word

5) Malta

Player   Country   Word

11) Bola Sepak

Player   Country   Word

6) Voetbal

Player   Country   Word

12) Tinga

Player   Country   Word

A record 204 nations will attempt to qualify for the **2010 World Cup**, up six from 2006. Bhutan is the only FIFA nation that hasn't entered the tournament.

Sudo Soccer

Answer the clues below, corresponding to their location in the grid on the following page. Each clue is answered with a number, and that number goes into the four locations listed in brackets. This is a sudoku grid, meaning each row, column and 3 × 3 grid must have the numbers one to nine in it exactly once. If you don't have every number once, you didn't answer the questions correctly! We've filled in a few numbers to start you off.

1) Max. number of yellow cards any player can receive in a game [A1, B9, C6, D4]

2) Max. number of substitutes allowed in pro soccer [C1, F3, H6, I2]

3) Number of flags on the field [B5, D8, G9, HI]

4) Number of shooters, per team, in a normal penalty shootout [A5, C9, F7, G8]

5) Number of gloves on the field during a typical game [A7, E3, F6, I4]

6) Common goalkeeper jersey number [A2, E5, F8, H9]

7) Goal kicks are taken from the __-yard line [A3, B4, F5, G2]

8) Ronaldo's jersey number [D6, E8, F1, G5]

9) Number of Canadian MLS teams [B6, C7, G4, I1]

10) Luis Figo's number [B1, E2, G6, H3]

11) Number of defensemen in a 3-5-2 formation [B8, D5, E9, G7]

12) Number of MLS Cups the San Jose Earthquakes have won, as of 2007 [E7, F2, G3, H5]

13) Kaka and Frank Lampard's jersey number [C3, D2, G1, H8]

14) Number of points Juventus was handicapped for the 2006–07 Serie B season, because of a match-fixing scandal [A9, C4, H2, I7]

Guinness record: The most touches of a ball in one minute, using only the head, is 319 by Cuban Erick Hernandez.

	1	2	3	4	5	6	7	8	9
A						8			
B			9						
C								6	
D	5								
E	6					5			
F				7					8
G									
H									
I					8		9		7

Bonus: Going back to 2000, who have been the last seven FIFA Players of the Year?

The Drop Hog Puzzle

Fill in the word in the middle to complete both soccer expressions or terms. For example, by adding the word "Game" to "Tie _____ Over," you get "Tie Game" and "Game Over."

1) Own _____ Kick

2) Drop _____ Hog

3) One - _____ on One

4) Cross _____ Time

5) Set _____ On

6) Off _____ Line

7) Free _____ Off

8) Silver _____ Difference

9) Through _____ Handling

10) Cruyff _____ Over

11) Top _____ Flag

12) Around the _____ Cup

13) Semi _____ Score

The **English Premier League** is televised in 152 countries. In 2005, it was watched in roughly 450 million homes, nearly one of every 12 people on earth.

26

First Things First

Soccer is likely the oldest sport in the world. Each question lists two historic events:
one soccer-related, the other something completely different. You must figure out
which happened first and circle your choice. Good luck!

1) A Major League Soccer played its first game.

B The Nintendo Entertainment System (NES) played its first game in 1983.

2) A FIFA was formed.

B The first TV show aired in 1928.

3) A Castleston State College became the first American school to establish a
varsity women's soccer program.

B In 1969, Neil Armstrong became the first man to walk on the moon.

4) A The first official Olympic soccer competition was held in London.

B Thomas Edison invented the light bulb in 1879.

5) A Jaime Moreno passed Jason Kreis as the all-time leading scorer in MLS.

B The world population reached 6.5 billion in 2006.

6) A Members of the Chinese military had to kick a small leather ball into a hole
as an exercise, the oldest documented evidence of soccer.

B Christians began counting years as Anno Domini, or AD, at year 1 AD. We are
currently in 2008 AD.

7) A The first-ever documented international match took place between England
and Scotland.

B The Wright Brothers built the first airplane to make a successful flight, in
1903.

8) A FIFA introduced the backpass rule, which states that a goalie may not pick up
a ball that has been passed to him by a player on his own team.

B *The Simpsons* debuted on TV in 1989.

AKA

Fill in the crossword grid. Most of the clues are synonyms for the answer, meaning the answer to each question is a word that means the same as the clue. For example, if the clue was "Match," the answer might be "Game." Good luck!

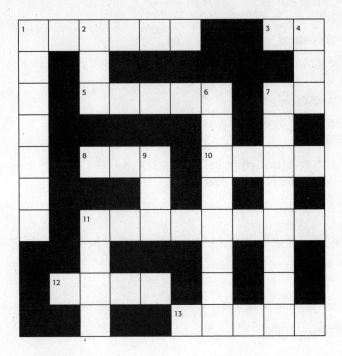

Across

1) Football

3) Penalty kick

5) Field

7) Overtime

8) Spectator

10) Weaker foot, commonly

11) Defender

12) Woodwork

13) Good ability

Down

1) Forward

2) Appearance in a game for your country

4) Equipment

6) Midfielder

7) Referee

9) Zero

11) Vital body part

As of 2007, Portuguese club Benfica has the most supporters in the world, with 160,398 paid members.

Ronaldo Who?

Can you match up these nicknames with the player's real name?
There are also a couple of national team nicknames in the puzzle.

Dida	Togo
Pele	Zinedine Zidane
The Blues	Ronaldo Luis Nazario de Lima
Ronaldinho	Fitz Hall
Kaka	Netherlands
One Size	Ronaldo de Assis Moreira
Sparrow Hawks	Edson Arantes do Nascimento
The Asian Maradona	Italy
The Divine Ponytail	Roberto Baggio
El Angel de Madrid	Nelson de Jesus Silva
The Truth	Ali Karimi
Azurri	Ricardo Izecson dos Santos Leite
Zizou	Raul Gonzalez
Ronaldo	France
Clockwork Orange	Kasey Keller

In 1967, Nigeria was in the middle of a brutal civil war,
but the two sides agreed on a 48-hour ceasefire so they could watch
Pele play an exhibition game in the capital city.

Round and Round Again

This puzzle goes in a spiral, starting with the top left corner and working around until all the spaces are filled up. The start of the next clue is formed by the last one or two letters of the previous answer. The number in brackets at the end of each clue gives the number of letters in the answer. Try working backwards if you get stuck.

1) Referee has this (7)

2) _____ - footed (4)

3) Challenge (6)

4) _____ Time (5)

5) Famous Scottish Club (also an NHL team) (7)

6) _____ Guards (4)

7) A free kick that cannot go directly into the goal (8)

8) Type of pass (requiring the player to run onto the ball) (7)

9) Only the goalie uses these (5)

10) Usually one or two of these on the field for each team (7)

11) Unlike baseball, there is no delay for this in soccer (4)

12) Many players fake this (6)

13) Ecuador/Sweden's main jersey color (6)

14) Michael _____ (English striker) (4)

15) Goalie guards this (3)

In 2006, Bulgarian **Ivelin Popov** was ordered by his club team to get married, on the grounds that he had too many girlfriends and partied too much. Popov, a member of Bulgaria's U-21 squad, promised to accept the order and find a wife.

Know Your Teams

1					2		
				8			3
	11		12				
				15			
7		14					
					13	9	
6			10				4
					5		

Bonus: What is commonly referred to as "The Hand of God"?

Know Your Teams

Can you guess which team these clues point towards? Use the box of teams on the adjacent page, and cross out each one as you fill them in.

1) This team brought a second country into the MLS mix.

   _____

2) This successful team has played at Old Trafford since 1910.

   _____

3) This team is named after all the stars in Hollywood.

   _____

4) These 2005–06 Champions League winners play out of Camp Nou, the largest stadium in Europe (98,918 capacity). As of 2006, they were the second-richest club in the world.

   _____

5) The first American club to win a tournament outside of North America, these former MetroStars should have no shortage of energy.

   _____

6) With four MLS Cup titles, this club is the most successful in league history.

   _____

7) The most successful club in Mexican league history, with 11 championships, this club has only ever fielded Mexican-born players.

   _____

8) In 2000, this club became the first in the world to win 100 trophies. They have won their domestic league 51 times since the league began play in 1890.

   _____

9) In 2006, this team won the USL First Division title (the league below MLS), and the women's team of the same name won the W-League title (the top women's league), a rare double-championship.

   _____

10) Scandalously, this team was relegated to Serie B after a match-fixing scandal in 2006.

_____

11) This team's name is made up of a part of the body, and a place you swim.

_____

12) FIFA named this club (known as Los Blancos) the best team of the 20th century.

_____

13) This club, one of the "Big Three" in Portugal, won the UEFA Cup in 2003 and Champions League the year after, a very rare accomplishment.

_____

14) With an estimated fan base of four million people, *The Blues* had a record season in 2004–05, recording the most points in Premiership history (95) and conceding the fewest goals (only 15). They won the Premiership again in 2005–06.

_____

15) The first and only French team to win the Champions League, this club has been struggling since the early nineties to regain its past glory.

_____

16) This team won the MLS Cup in 2006, their first year in the league (though they used to be the San Jose Earthquakes). They successfully defended the title in 2007, becoming the second repeat winners in MLS history.

_____

17) In 2006, these Gunners became the first London-based team to make the Champions League final.

_____

Arsenal FC	Manchester United	FC Porto
Chelsea FC	Los Angeles Galaxy	Juventus FC
Vancouver Whitecaps	New York Red Bulls	DC United
Houston Dynamo	Toronto FC	Liverpool FC
Real Madrid	FC Barcelona	FC Rangers
Olympique de Marseille	Club Deportivo Guadalajara	

Through Ball #2

Each of these random rows of letters has a soccer-related term or name hidden within. Fill in the one missing letter in the centre to reveal the word. For example, with "FONTESOC ___ ERBASINS," add a C to the centre to reveal "Soccer."

1)   GRIMBONA ___ EFEREENY

2)   KEALOOFF ___ IDECANOP

3)   MBADAVID ___ ECKHAMME

4)   LAMAZOTH ___ NDBALLET

5)   SHARSHAF ___ EEKICKMO

6)   OSHALFTI ___ EMINCEVO

7)   NESKICKO ___ FEMARIOW

8)   UNRECAPT ___ INAKARTH

9)   PASWHIST ___ ELMOELMO

10) REBICYCL ___ KICKLENT

11) TRIGHTFO ___ TENEASHO

12) RARGOALI ___ ALINTTER

13) ASOTHIER ___ YHENRYOU

Bonus: As of 2007, who are the top five all-time leading goal scorers at the World Cup?

Who Am I? #2

See if you can figure out who these clues point towards, in the fewest clues possible.

1) I wore number 11.
2) I am one of only four players who have scored in two different World Cup finals.
3) I retired in 2006, after being named the Best Player of the World Cup that year.
4) I have been sent off 14 times in my career, most notably in extra time during the 2006 World Cup final.

Who am I?_____

1) I was born October 30, 1960.
2) I played in four different World Cups.
3) I scored the "Goal of the Century" in 1986, the same year I won the World Cup.
4) I am one of the most controversial players in history, and in 2000 I was named the best player in history after an online FIFA poll, making Argentina proud.

Who am I?_____

1) I was born in Porto Alegre, in March 1980.
2) In January 2007, I became a Spanish citizen. I have a line of clothing called "R10."
3) Before joining FC Barcelona in 2003, I played with Paris Saint-Germain and Gremio.
4) I won consecutive FIFA Player of the Year awards in 2004 and 2005, but failed to lead Brazil past the quarter-finals in World Cup 2006.

Who am I?_____

As of 2007, players from the **United States** have the most international caps among men (nine players over 100) and women (18 over 100) of any nation.

Substitutes

The players' names below are listed according to their length. Fit them into their proper place in the grid; there is only one correct place for each word. To start you off, we filled in the letter A. Now, find a four-letter word with A as the second letter.

4 Letters
Cafu
Kone
Noor
Oddo

5 Letters
Dudic
Dudka
Eboue
Kader
Kovac
Lewis
Mares
Ochoa
Reina

6 Letters
Essien
Kewell
Lennon
Onyewu
Timmer
Zidane

7 Letters
Cabanas
Caneira
Koroman
Nilsson
Romaric
Shaaban

8 Letters
Arellano
Azofeifa
Drummond
Elmander
Kromkamp
Martinez
Saritama
Sequeria
Takahara

In 1982, **Laszlo Kiss** of El Salvador made history, becoming the first (and only) substitute to score a World Cup hat trick. Remarkably, he did it in only seven minutes (scoring at 67, 72 and 76 minutes).

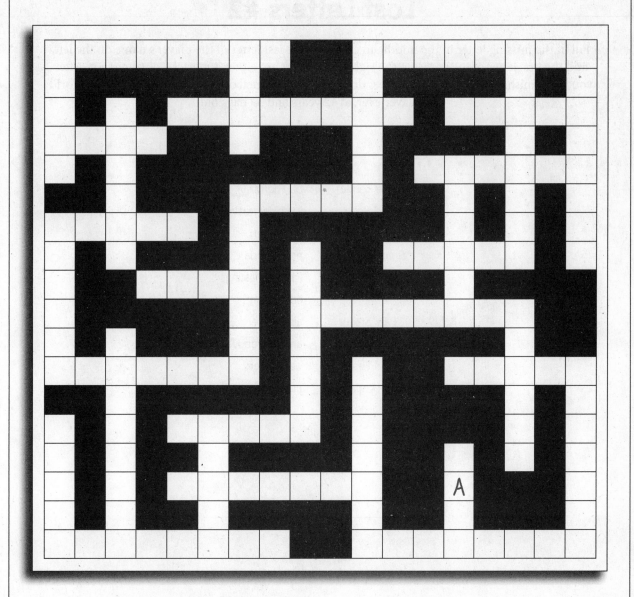

Bonus: Of the 22 FIFA World Cups, men's and women's, how many times has the host country won? A) 0; B) 2; C) 7; D) 12

Lost Letters #2

Fill in the missing letter in the middle to complete the last letter of the player's name on the left, and the first letter of the name on the right. All players are either American or Canadian. After you have finished each name, the letters down the middle spell out the name of the oldest World Cup player ever, at 42 years and 39 days old.

Patrice Bernie	___	ob Friend
Dwayne De Rosari	___	wen Hargreaves
Chad Deerin	___	reg Sutton
Brian McBrid	___	ric Wynalda
Kasey Kelle	___	ichard Shastings
Jeff Cunningha	___	artin Nash
Paul Stalter	___	ain Hume
Bobby Boswel	___	andon Donovan
Brad Friede	___	ee Nguyen
Carlos Bocanegr	___	tiba Hutchinson

Oldest player:

_____

Bonus: Which countries have been in the last five UEFA European Championship finals, going back to 1988? Who won?

Sounds Like

These famous players' names have been mixed up and replaced with words that rhyme. We've filled in one to start you off. Try saying them out loud if you get stuck!

1)	Real-Cheapo In-Baggie	=	Filippo Inzaghi
2)	Save-It Deck-Him	=	_____
3)	Plain Looney	=	_____
4)	Tea-Rarely On Me	=	_____
5)	Eat Her Couch	=	_____
6)	Go-Waldo	=	_____
7)	On-Play Rev-Then-Go	=	_____
8)	Leavin' Their-Yard	=	_____
9)	Donald-Mean-Yo	=	_____
10)	Ready Apu	=	_____
11)	Snafu	=	_____
12)	Spyin' Biggs	=	_____
13)	Tao-Know All-Teenie	=	_____
14)	Fafa	=	_____
15)	Rank Jam-Dart	=	_____
16)	Neck-o	=	_____
17)	Gone Very	=	_____
18)	Neo-Gel Jesse	=	_____
19)	Mowin' Our-Leaves	=	_____

Players from 48 different national leagues played in **World Cup 2006**, with the most coming from England's Premier League (102), Germany's Bundesliga (74) and Italy's Serie A (60). In total, there were 736 players.

More Hidden Players

The last names below have been hidden in the grid, starting with the central letter D and extending out. The letters can be connected on either side, above, below or diagonally. The same letter cannot be used twice in the same name. Watch out, two of the names listed below are not actually hidden in the puzzle. Can you figure out which two?

N	G	M	I	I	O	V
I	A	R	E	N	A	N
N	W	L	Y	O	F	D
A	B	O	D	E	N	O
G	L	E	A	I	G	L
A	D	R	C	D	N	O
O	R	O	G	T	E	S

Names

Christian DAILLY
Craig DARGO
DECO
Augustin DELGADO
Jermain DEFOE
Alou DIARRA

Nicolae DICA
DIDA
DIEGO
Aruna DINDANE
Siza DLAMINI
Andreas DOBER

DONI
Landon DONOVAN
Stewart DOWNING
Michael DOYLE
Didier DROGBA
Kieron DYER

The **2006 World Cup** was broadcast by a record 500 different channels worldwide, nearly doubling the number in 2002. The FIFA website generated a record 4.2 billion views during the competition.

Word Work

See how many words you can make using only the letters in "Champion." They must be three letters or longer. Proper names don't count. Then, see how many words you can make using only the letters in "Football." Which one is hiding more words?

CHAMPION

_____ _____ _____
_____ _____ _____
_____ _____ _____
_____ _____ _____
_____ _____ _____
_____ _____ _____
_____ _____ _____
_____ _____ _____

FOOTBALL

_____ _____ _____
_____ _____ _____
_____ _____ _____
_____ _____ _____
_____ _____ _____
_____ _____ _____
_____ _____ _____

American **Kristine Lilly** has appeared in 330 international games, a record for both men and women. As of 2007, she had played in about 85 percent of the USA's international matches.

Quotables

See if you can pick the true quote, avoiding the two made-up ones.

1) **Pele, in his autobiography:**
   A) "I dedicate this book to all the people who have made this great game the Beautiful Game."
   B) "Dedicated to my right foot, the divine chalice of the Gods."
   C) "I dedicate this book to the goalkeepers I have beaten. Thank you."

2) **Tarciso Burgnich, on marking Pele at the 1970 World Cup:**
   A) "I thought he was made of flesh and bone like me. I was wrong."
   B) "That was the worst day of my life."
   C) "Frankly, I don't know what the big deal is. Pele has minimal skills."

3) **Mark Draper, on Italian teams:**
   A) "Ninnies, nincompoops and hollywoppers."
   B) "I'd like to play for an Italian club, like Barcelona."
   C) "Italy has a square mile circumference of 200 million soccer balls."

4) **Actor Antonio Banderas, on soccer:**
   A) "I was playing with a soccer team in Spain until I broke my foot — badly. That's when I started seriously getting into acting."
   B) "During the filming of *Zorro*, I was so busy I missed the World Cup. That was the worst thing that has happened in my acting career."
   C) "During the day, I act on screen. In my dreams, I play on the field."

5) **Freddy Adu, on himself:**
   A) "I'm young. I don't know myself very well, but we have a lot of time to develop a better relationship."
   B) "I am not just Freddy Adu … I am the millions of young guys who want to play soccer professionally. I am a dream."
   C) "Sometimes I even amaze myself, and sometimes I do things that make me want to punch myself in the face."

6) **Michael Owen, on food:**
   A) "I don't even know how to make a cup of tea or coffee. I can boil a kettle for a pot noodle, and I've been known to warm up some food in the microwave, but cookery is definitely not one of my specialties."
   B) "I always eat mashed potatoes before a game. Makes me play better."
   C) "Before I visited America, I thought a waffle was one of those contests where you win money."

7) **David Beckham, on his family:**

   A) "My family is the billions of people cheering for my team."

   B) "My family have been there for me, ever since I was about seven."

   C) "I love Posh Spice, she is an essential spice, like paprika."

8) **Sven-Goran Eriksson (England's former manager), on David Beckham:**

   A) "David Beckham should think that talking is silver, but being quiet is golden."

   B) "I talked to him about his weird haircuts, because my son always wants to copy them. I told him to think of the children."

   C) "He is a super star. England only needs a star."

9) **Mia Hamm, on winning:**

   A) "I win so the other team doesn't have to."

   B) "Confidence takes constant nurturing. Like a bed, it must be remade every day."

   C) "There's no 'I' in 'win'."

10) **Ian Rush, on living in Italy:**

   A) "I couldn't settle in Italy – it was like living in a foreign country."

   B) "I am English. They were Italians. We're not Englians or Italish."

   C) "I have had a successful career. I deserve a place where my only worry is which brand of sunscreen to buy."

11) **Alan Shearer, on Newcastle:**

   A) "I bleed black and white stripes."

   B) "I am a king, and this is my castle."

   C) "I've never wanted to leave. I'm here for the rest of my life, and hopefully after that as well."

12) **George Weah, on Sundays:**

   A) "Sunday is the Holy Day, when all religions come together on the field. The ball is our god."

   B) "George Weah loves soccer. George Weah loves Sundays."

   C) "It can't be Sunday every day. There are also Mondays and Tuesdays."

13) **Ronaldo, on naming his son:**

   A) "Choosing a name is the hardest thing I have ever done."

   B) "He will be called Ronald, because we like going to McDonald's."

   C) "My wife wanted to name him Palosandro, so I said, why not just name him 'child with bad name'?"

In 2007, Brazilian **Romario** became the second player to score 1,000 career goals in pro soccer. He did it at age 41, while it only took Pele 29 years. There is some controversy though, as Romario includes his amateur goals, which FIFA does not count.

Game On

Fill in the crossword grid by answering each clue, corresponding to the number in the grid.

Across

1) Hitting the ball with the back of your foot

4) This Cup is the oldest soccer tournament in the world

5) ____CACAF (Organization that holds the Gold Cup, North America's premier trophy)

6) Sweet spot on the shoe

8) Abbreviation for the person formerly called "linesman"

10) Type of (offensive) midfielder

13) It's helpful if a goalie has a strong one of these

14) Striking the ball while it's in the air

16) Carded players go in this

18) In theory, it's not a foul if the defender gets ____ of the ball

20) A pass back, or a type of kick

21) New home of the player from 1 Down

Down

1) Many players wish they could bend it like _____

2) Fabio _____ (2006 FIFA Player of the Year)

3) 45-minute mark

4) Found in the corner

7) Guard, protect

11) Providing defensive support, or another word for mark (as in marking a player)

12) "___ Ball!"

15) It's still a "hand" ball if the ball touches this

16) Essential for soccer

17) Star Brazilian midfielder, plays for AC Milan

19) Champions League rounds have a first and second _____

Guinness record: The longest time heading a ball without letting it drop is eight hours and 32 minutes, set by Swede Tomas Lundman in 2004.

Bonus: As of 2008, only 21 men have scored in three different World Cups, and only five players have scored twice from direct free kicks. Which player joined both groups in 2006?

The Fung a Wing Puzzle

There could be a whole book on the wacky names in soccer. For this puzzle, can you spot the four made-up names from the list below?

Roberto Perfumo	Poo Doo Ik
Cilly Foreshore	Naughty Mokoena
Gilles Yapi Yapo	Laughter Chilembe
Razak Pimpong	Fastah Slurpah
Jan Vennegoor of Hesselink	Suprise Moriri
Hakan Yakin	Harry B. Daft
Shaka Hislop	Cheesy Pops
Stern Westminstersunningson	Jimmy Zakazaka
Cerezo Fung a Wing	Danger Fourpence
Creedence Clearwater Couto	Joseph-Desire Job
Bongo Christ	Johnny Moustache

The longest name in pro soccer belongs to Anthony Philip David Terry Frank Donald Stanley Gerry Gordon Stephen James Oatway, known as **Charlie Oatway** to his friends. Named after the 11 starting players on the Queens Park Rangers 1972 team, Oatway plays for Football League One squad Brighton & Hove Albion FC.

Scrambled Countries

The names of these soccer nations have been all mixed up. Can you unscramble them all? Watch out, each clue has one extra letter thrown in to confuse you. These 13 extra letters can be unscrambled to spell another country. Good luck.

1) Lcrizab   _____

2) Gantiarenp   _____

3) Bugltrapo   _____

4) Ancajp   _____

5) Mkanirde   _____

6) Danegrln   _____

7) Margyezn   _____

8) Ecmoexi   _____

9) Clatyi   _____

10) Ranchef   _____

11) Esau   _____

12) Calnaad   _____

13) Punsai   _____

Bonus: As of 2007, FIFA has awarded the Women's World Player of the Year trophy six times. Can you name the winner for each year, going back to 2001? Hint: only three different women have won.

Sudo Soccer #2

Answer the clues below, corresponding to their location in the grid on the following page. Each clue is answered with a number, and that number goes into the four locations listed in brackets. This is a sudoku grid, meaning each row, column and 3 × 3 grid must have the numbers one to nine in it exactly once. If you don't have every number once, you didn't answer the questions correctly! We've filled in a few numbers to start you off.

1) Number of players involved in a give-and-go [A3, D6, E1, H2]

2) Number of forwards in a 5-2-3 formation [C5, F6, H9, I4]

3) Total number of medals awarded at the 2008 Olympics in soccer [D9, G8, H5, I1]

4) Only touching the ball a single time is known as __ - touch [A5, E4, G2, I6]

5) David Beckham's jersey number [A1, B6, E9, G5]

6) Number of white spots on a typical field [A8, B2, D7, E3]

7) Cristiano Ronaldo's jersey number [C7, D3, F4, H8]

8) 199__ World Cup, held in the United States [C8, D4, E7, G6]

9) Total number of goals in a "5-nil aggregate" [A6, E8, G4, H3]

10) Number of groups in the first round of the World Cup [C2, G3, H6, I8]

11) The first Women's World Cup was held in China, in 19_1 [A9, C6, F8, G7]

12) Number of Women's World Cups, as of 2009 [B9, D2, F5, I7]

13) As of 2008, number of World Cup appearances for Canada's men's team [B3, C9, F1, H7]

14) As of 2008, number of World Cup appearances for the USA's men's team [A4, B7, D1, E5]

As of 2008, there have been **48 hat tricks** in 700+ men's World Cup games. The 2006 tournament was the only one without a hat trick scored.

	1	2	3	4	5	6	7	8	9
A									
B					4				
C			6						
D								1	
E		9				6			
F									8
G									2
H	4			9					
I		7							

Bonus: Rank these players according to their age, from youngest to oldest: Ronaldo, Ronaldinho, David Beckham, Mia Hamm, Cristiano Ronaldo and Marta.

More Choice

Can you pick the correct answer?

1) As of 2007, only three countries have ever been ranked first or second on the FIFA Women's World Rankings. What are the three countries?
   A) Norway, Denmark and Sweden
   B) Argentina, Brazil and the USA
   C) Canada, China and the USA
   D) The USA, Germany and Norway

2) According to David Beckham, if he wasn't a soccer player, what would his profession of choice have been?
   A) Astronaut
   B) Hairdresser
   C) Model
   D) Comedian

3) Why did India withdraw from their first and only World Cup, in 1950?
   A) Because FIFA would not allow them to play barefoot.
   B) Because half the players didn't know where the World Cup was being held (nine players showed up in France, leaving only eight players in Brazil).
   C) Their team all came down with chicken pox.
   D) Because, according to their manager Sandeep Nanji, "It was far too cold."

4) Where is the largest soccer stadium in the world, with a capacity of 150,000?
   A) Mexico City
   B) Pyongang, North Korea
   C) Kolkata, India
   D) London, England

5) What is Futsol?
   A) Indoor soccer. FIFA holds Futsol World Cups, featuring 5–5 play with lines as outs.
   B) Pronounced "Foots-all," it is the term coined by Dario Milaneti to describe the world appeal of soccer/football. It was awarded the 2007 Merriam-Webster "Word of the Year."
   C) A skillful soccer move that involves balancing the ball on top of your head while running.
   D) A rap group from the Czech Republic. They have released four albums as of 2008, and every track features rhymes about soccer.

Guinness record: The most touches of a ball in 30 seconds, while keeping the ball airborne, is 147 by American Tim Crowe.

6) Just before the 1966 World Cup in England, the World Cup trophy was stolen from an exhibition display. How was the trophy recovered?

    A) FIFA paid a $9 million ransom for it. The thief was never identified.

    B) A dog named Pickles found it under some bushes in London.

    C) French goalie Marcel Aubour found it floating in the Thames.

    D) A naked man ran onto the field during the opening game of the tournament, clutching the trophy. He was tackled by security.

7) At the 2007 FIFA U20 World Cup, what did the Czech Republic have to do between their semi-final game and the final?

    A) Travel 3,468 kilometres (2,155 miles).

    B) Play two tie-breakers, because the quarter-final penalty kick shootout against Italy was disputed. The first tie-breaker was cancelled midway through because of lightning, but they finally beat Italy in Game Three.

    C) Get hypnotized. Miroslave Soukup, their coach, took them to a hypnotist for a marathon 18-hour session. One player described the experience as "… the strangest day of my life."

    D) Buy new jerseys, because their only set of shirts was washed with a red towel, and came out pink.

8) What became an international incident after Chile's U20 World Cup loss to Argentina in the semi-finals?

    A) A naked man ran on the field in the 93rd minute, causing the game to be called one minute early, much to the dismay of the Chileans.

    B) Angered by the refereeing, Chilean players trashed their team bus and reportedly fought with police. No charges were laid.

    C) Argentina's winning goal, the only one in the game, clearly did not cross the goal line after video review. The goal stood, giving Argentina the win.

    D) All of the above.

9) What strange soccer tournament was held at Georgia Tech University in 2007?

    A) The Three-Legged Dog Cup.

    B) The Wee-Baby World Cup. All players had to be 12 months old or younger.

    C) The 7th-Annual Longest Volley Kick Off.

    D) The RoboCup 2007, with over 300 teams from 37 countries. The organizers hope to, by 2050, "Develop a team of fully autonomous humanoid robots that can win against the human world champion team."

10) Germany defeated Brazil to win the 2007 Women's World Cup. In the process, they became the first senior team (men's or women's) at a major tournament to do what?

    A) Not allow a goal.

    B) Allow more goals (9) than they scored (6).

    C) Score only from penalty kicks.

    D) Live together for the three months prior to the World Cup. The entire German team stayed in a house with 18 rooms, five bathrooms, a pool table, a Jacuzzi and an indoor soccer arena.

What Am I? #2

See if you can figure out what these clues point towards, in as few clues as possible.

1) I'm almost always debated.
2) I often come with a card.
3) I usually result in a goal.
4) I'm taken from 12 yards.

What am I?_____

1) I'm mandatory.
2) I go on first.
3) The ball might take a strange bounce if it comes off me.
4) I come in different shapes and sizes, but I always protect.

What am I?_____

1) I stop play.
2) I can't happen before the half-way line.
3) I often make players stick up their arm.
4) I often come from through balls, and give the assistant referee some work.

What am I?_____

> Miroslav Klose won the **Golden Shoe** award for most goals at the 2006 World Cup, with five. That was the lowest number of goals for a winner since 1962.

More Hidden Countries

Ten countries are hidden below, starting with the central letter C and extending out. The letters can be connected on either side, above, below or diagonally. The same letter cannot be used twice in the same name. All countries have played in the World Cup at least once. How many can you find?

D	A	E	R	O	O	N
A	I	N	M	C	I	L
C	B	H	A	H	E	R
I	L	U	C	R	S	A
E	P	E	Z	O	T	I
R	I	C	A	N	L	B
A	H	T	O	G	M	O

Bonus: 13 teams played in MLS in 2007. How many can you name?

Lost Ladies

The last names of 22 women's soccer stars are hidden below. They are written forwards or backwards, and are hidden diagonally, horizontally and vertically. After you've crossed out each name, the leftover letters spell out the name of the first woman offered a contract by a major men's league team (Serie A club Perugia Calcio).

H	G	Z	N	I	R	P	S	B	M
I	A	N	R	G	E	D	R	S	U
B	I	M	A	F	P	Y	E	I	R
N	E	T	M	L	O	O	K	N	R
I	L	N	P	E	O	L	A	C	A
A	I	G	G	E	H	L	T	L	Y
T	L	L	R	T	L	R	R	A	N
S	L	R	I	I	S	E	A	I	O
A	Y	M	M	N	N	S	M	R	H
H	S	C	E	G	G	O	I	C	
C	A	W	A	S	N	O	S	N	I
M	E	D	A	L	E	N	R	Z	P

Names

Michelle AKERS
Kristin BENGTSSON
Brandi CHASTAIN
Julie FLEETING
Inka GRINGS
Mia HAMM
Charmaine HOOPER
Kara LANG

Kristine LILLY
Renate LINGOR
Carli LLOYD
Shannon MACMILLAN
MARTA
Linda MEDALEN
Julie MURRAY
Marinette PICHON

Birgit PRINZ
Hege RIISE
Homare SAWA
Christine SINCLAIR
Kelly SMITH
Sun WEN

First woman offered a contract : __ __ __ __ __ __   __ __ __ __ __

p. 1: **The Great Search**

R	C	A	N	N	A	V	A	R	O
F	O	C	R	U	Y	F	F	I	N
M	V	N	**A**	**B**	**I**	O	G	E	O
A	O	H	A	E	W	G	W	K	V
T	N	Z	O	L	A	O	N	F	O
T	A	I	D	B	D	E	**C**	I	K
H	L	D	L	L	H	I	R	G	H
A	E	A	A	C	**A**	A	N	O	C
U	B	N	V	**N**	M	**N**	I	H	I
S	O	E	I	O	**A**	V	P	**A**	O
R	H	**R**	R	E	M	M	A	S	T
S	N	E	D	V	E	D	P	**O**	S

The leftover letters spell Fabio Cannavaro.

p. 2: **Finish the Cross**

Across
1) Italy
2) Spain
5) Jump
9) Bicycle
11) Red
12) Free
13) Hands
15) Green
17) On
18) Chip
19) Madrid
22) Inter
23) Slide

Down
1) Injury
3) Play
4) In
6) Midfield
7) Give
8) Head
10) Champions
14) Send
15) Games
16) FC
20) Ice
21) Set

Bonus: Arsenal, Aston Villa, Birmingham City, Blackburn Rovers, Bolton Wanderers, Chelsea, Derby County, Everton, Fulham, Liverpool, Manchester City, Manchester United, Middlesbrough, Newcastle United, Portsmouth, Reading, Sunderland, Tottenham Hotspur, West Ham United, Wigan Athletic.

p. 4: **Your Choice**

1) A
2) C
3) A
4) A
5) C
6) B
7) A
8) D
9) B (The organization was formed by 14 teams, and four others have joined since.)
10) D

p. 6: **Lost Letters**

Gianluigi Buffo **N** wankwo Kanu
Romari **O** liver Kahn
Gerd Mulle **R** aul Gonzalez
Philip Lah **M** ichael Bradley
Gabriel Batistut **A** ndriy Shevchenko
Arjen Robbe **N** icolas Burdisso
John Care **W** ayne Rooney
Petr Cec **H** ernan Crespo
Luca Ton **I** van Zamarano
Dirk Kuy **T** hierry Henry
Pel **E** ddie Pope
Jeff Agoo **S** amuel Eto'o
Ali Dae **I** van Hurtado
Pavel Nedve **D** idier Drogba
Miroslav Klos **E** ric Wynalda

The letters down the middle spell Norman Whiteside.

Bonus: B) 11 seconds

p. 7: **Who Am I?**

A) Freddy Adu
B) Mia Hamm
C) Peter Schmeichel

p. 8: **Through Ball**

1) V – Stepover
2) D – Maradona
3) R – World Cup
4) B – Backpass
5) O – Goalpost
6) T – Tackle
7) W – Throw In
8) T – Striker
9) A – Header
10) D – Shinpads
11) O – Corner
12) Y – Penalty
13) R – Red Card

p. 9: **Confused Clubs**

Tottenham Hotspur FC – English Premier League
FC Barcelona – La Liga
Olympique Lyonnais – Ligue 1
FC Bayern Munich – Bundesliga
AS Roma – Italian Serie A
Celtic FC – Scottish Premier League
DC United – Major League Soccer
Kashima Antlers – J-League Division 1
Club Deportivo Guadalajara – Primera Division de Mexico
AFC Ajax – Eredivisie
FC Spartak Moscow – Russian Premier League
FC Dynamo Kyiv – Ukrainian Premier League
SL Benfica – Portuguese Liga
Club Atletico Boca Juniors – Primera Division Argentina

Bonus: The most cards, with 16 yellows and four reds. The Netherlands had seven yellows and two reds, while Portugal had nine cautions and two reds.

p. 10: **Round and Round**

1) Friendly
2) Yellow
3) Own
4) Net
5) Trap
6) Penalty
7) Yards
8) Step
9) EPL
10) Landon
11) On Side
12) Denmark
13) Kit
14) Time
15) England
16) Dribble

p. 12: **The Transfer**

1) Hand – Band – Bald – Ball
2) Shoe – Shot – Soot – Boot
3) Start – Stare – Scare – Score
4) Chip – Ship – Shop – Shot
5) Best – Pest – Past – Pass
6) Pele – Pile – Pine – Wine – Wins
7) Post – Lost – List – Lint – Line
8) Foot – Fort – Ford – Cord – Card

Note: There may be more than one way to solve these correctly.

Soccer is the world's most popular sport. According to FIFA, there are **over 240 million players** on 1.4 million teams and 300,000 clubs across the world.

p. 13: **Hidden Players**

SAPULA and SANCHEZ are not in the puzzle.

Bonus: Gianluigi Buffon. He was transferred to Juventus from Parma FC in 2001, for roughly US$63 million. Buffon was signed at age 17 by Parma, in 1995.

p. 14: **What Am I?**

A) The World Cup Trophy
B) The FIFA Women's World Cup
C) Bicycle Kick

p. 15: **World of Soccer**

Men:

1) Brazil
2) Italy
3) Germany
4) Argentina
   Uruguay
5) France
   England

Women:

1) USA
   Germany
2) Norway

p. 16: **The Starting Lineup**

Bonus: Australia, Argentina, Brazil, Canada, China PR, Denmark, England, Germany, Ghana, Japan, Korea DPR, New Zealand, Nigeria, Norway, Sweden and the USA.

p. 18: **True or False**

1) True
2) True
3) True
4) False
5) True
6) False
7) False
8) True
9) True
10) False
11) False
12) False
13) True
14) True
15) True

p. 20: **Spot the Fake**

Figaro Figazio, ACFCNA, Volley and Horkin Famplo are fake.

p. 21: **Missing Leaders**

S	T	A	L	Y	A	N	I	B	**R**
A	**A**	N	O	T	L	R	A	H	C
K	**U**	P	V	**L**	T	A	A	L	L
S	**G**	R	E	E	I	**O**	B	N	L
U	E	N	U	S	L	D	D	E	E
P	O	N	T	I	U	E	U	S	D
B	**N**	U	A	L	M	**Z**	L	L	Y
D	T	**A**	L	M	U	L	L	E	R
A	N	A	A	**L**	U	**E**	A	I	U
E	H	H	S	U	R	A	H	N	K
I	O	H	A	S	S	A	N	**Z**	U
M	J	R	E	L	L	O	K	G	S

The leftover letters spell Raul Gonzalez.

Bonus: Majed Abdullah – Saudi Arabia, Bashar Abdullah – Kuwait, Gabriel Batistuta – Italy, Hristo Bonev – Bulgaria, Bobby Charlton – England, Ali Daei – Iran, Hossam Hassan – Egypt, Stern John – Trinidad & Tobago, Jan Koller – Czech Republic, Kazuyoshi Miura – Japan, Hussain Saeed Mohammed – Iraq, Gerd Muller – Germany, Poul Nielsen – Denmark, Pele – Brazil, Ferenc Puskas – Hungary, Ian Rush – Wales, Sven Rydell – Sweden, Kiatisuk Senamuang – Thailand, Hakan Sukur – Turkey, Adnan Al Talyani – United Arab Emirates.

p. 22: **Hidden Countries**

The countries are: Saudi Arabia, Scotland, Senegal, Serbia, Slovenia, South Africa, South Korea, Spain, Sweden and Switzerland.

Bonus: 2006: Italy 1 – France 1, Italy won 5–3 on PKs; 2002: Brazil 2 – Germany 0; 1998: France 3 – Brazil 0; 1994: Brazil 0 – Italy 0, Brazil won 3–2 on PKs; 1990: West Germany 1 – Argentina 0.

In 2002, Madagascan club team **Stade Olympique l'Emryne** scored 149 own goals in the final game of the season, as a protest to what they felt was unfair refereeing in the league. The other team reportedly only touched the ball at the opening kickoff.

p. 23: **Back to Basics**

1) Country
2) Word (Italian)
3) Player
4) Country
5) Country
6) Word (Dutch)
7) Country
8) Player
9) Word (Croatian)
10) Player
11) Word (Malay)
12) Player

p. 24: **Sudo Soccer**

	1	2	3	4	5	6	7	8	9
A	2	1	6	3	5	8	4	7	9
B	7	5	9	6	4	1	8	3	2
C	3	4	8	9	7	2	1	6	5
D	5	8	1	2	3	9	7	4	6
E	6	7	4	8	1	5	2	9	3
F	9	2	3	7	6	4	5	1	8
G	8	6	2	1	9	7	3	5	4
H	4	9	7	5	2	3	6	8	1
I	1	3	5	4	8	6	9	2	7

Bonus: 2006: Fabio Cannavaro; 2005: Ronaldinho; 2004: Ronaldinho; 2003: Zinedine Zidane; 2002: Ronaldo; 2001: Luis Figo; 2000: Zinedine Zidane.

p. 26: **The Drop Hog Puzzle**

1) Goal
2) Ball
3) Two
4) Over
5) Play
6) Side
7) Kick
8) Goal
9) Ball
10) Turn
11) Corner
12) World
13) Final

p. 27: **First Things First**

1) B
2) A
3) A
4) B
5) A
6) A
7) A
8) B

p. 28: **AKA**

Across		Down	
1)	Soccer	1)	Striker
3)	PK	2)	Cap
5)	Pitch	4)	Kit
7)	OT	6)	Halfback
8)	Fan	7)	Official
10)	Left	9)	Nil
11)	Fullback	11)	Foot
12)	Post		
13)	Skill		

p. 29: **Ronaldo Who?**

Dida – Nelson de Jesus Silva
Pele – Edson Arantes do Nascimento
The Blues – France
Ronaldinho – Ronaldo de Assis Moreira
Kaka – Ricardo Izecson dos Santos Leite
One Size – Fitz Hall
Sparrow Hawks – Togo
The Asian Maradona – Ali Karimi
The Divine Ponytail – Roberto Baggio
El Angel de Madrid – Raul Gonzalez
The Truth – Kasey Keller
Azurri – Italy
Zizou – Zinedine Zidane
Ronaldo – Ronaldo Luis Nazario de Lima
Clockwork Orange – Netherlands

p. 30: **Round and Round Again**

1) Whistle
2) Left
3) Tackle
4) Extra
5) Rangers
6) Shin
7) Indirect
8) Through
9) Hands
10) Striker
11) Rain
12) Injury
13) Yellow
14) Owen
15) Net

Bonus: "The Hand of God" refers to a goal that Diego Maradona scored in the 1986 World Cup quarter-final against England, when the Argentine star struck the ball into the goal with his hand. Undetected by the ref, the goal was allowed, and Argentina won 2–1. In a post-game interview, Maradona stated the goal was scored "a little with the head of Maradona and a little with the Hand of God."

p. 32: **Know Your Teams**

1) Toronto FC
2) Manchester United
3) Los Angeles Galaxy
4) FC Barcelona
5) New York Red Bulls
6) DC United
7) Club Deportivo Guadalajara
8) FC Rangers
9) Vancouver Whitecaps
10) Juventus
11) Liverpool FC
12) Real Madrid
13) FC Porto
14) Chelsea FC
15) Olympique de Marseille
16) Houston Dynamo
17) Arsenal FC

p. 34: **Through Ball #2**

1) R – Referee
2) S – Offside
3) B – David Beckham
4) A – Handball
5) R – Freekick
6) M – Halftime
7) F – Kickoff
8) A – Captain
9) L – Whistle
10) E – Bicycle Kick
11) O – Right Foot
12) E – Goalie
13) R – Thierry Henry

Bonus: #1 Ronaldo (15), #2 Gerd Muller (14), #3 Just Fontaine (13), #4 Pele (12), #5 Jurgen Klinsmann & Sandor Kocsis (10)

p. 35: **Who Am I? #2**

A) Zinedine Zidane
B) Diego Maradona
C) Ronaldinho

p. 36: **Substitutes**

Bonus: C) 7

In **Pele's first World Cup** in 1958, he scored a hat trick against France in the semi-final and added two more in the final, becoming the youngest player to score in the Cup, let alone in the final. At the time, he was also the youngest player ever, at 17 years and 230 days old.

p. 38: Lost Letters #2

Patrice Bernie **R** ob Friend
Dwayne De Rosari **O** wen Hargreaves
Chad Deerin **G** reg Sutton
Brian McBrid **E** ric Wynalda
Kasey Kelle **R** ichard Shastings
Jeff Cunningha **M** artin Nash
Paul Stalter **I** ain Hume
Bobby Boswel **L** andon Donovan
Brad Friede **L** ee Nguyen
Carlos Bocanegr **A** tiba Hutchinson

The letters down the middle spell Roger Milla.

Bonus: 2004: Greece 1 – Portugal 0; 2000: France 2 – Italy 1; 1996: Germany 2 – Czech Republic 1; 1992: Denmark 2 – Germany 0; 1988: Netherlands 2 – USSR 0

p. 39: Sounds Like

2) David Beckham
3) Wayne Rooney
4) Thierry Henry
5) Peter Crouch
6) Ronaldo
7) Andriy Chevchenko
8) Steven Gerrard
9) Ronaldinho
10) Freddy Adu
11) Cafu
12) Ryan Giggs
13) Paolo Maldini
14) Kaka
15) Frank Lampard
16) Deco
17) John Terry
18) Lionel Messi
19) Owen Hargreaves

p. 40: More Hidden Players

DAILLY and DROGBA are not in the puzzle.

p. 41: Word Work

Champion – 37 words

Amp	Chomp	Mach	Pinch
Camp	Chop	Main	Imp
Can	Coin	Man	Inca
Cap	Coma	Map	Inch
Chain	Con	Moan	Ion
Chap	Cop	Mop	Nap
Chin	Ham	Pain	Nip
China	Him	Pan	
Chip	Hip	Pica	
Chimp	Hop	Pin	

Football – 36 words

Aft	Boll	Foal	Oaf
All	Fool	Bolt	Oat
Aloft	Foot	Boo	Taboo
Aloof	Lab	Boot	Tall
Alto	Loaf	Fall	Tab
Ball	Lob	Fat	Tao
Bat	Loft	Flab	Toll
Boa	Loot	Flat	Too
Boat	Lot	Float	Tool

p. 42: Quotables

1)	A	8)	A
2)	A	9)	B
3)	B	10)	A
4)	A	11)	C
5)	C	12)	C
6)	A	13)	B
7)	B		

p. 44: Game On

Across		Down	
1)	Backheel	1)	Beckham
4)	FA	2)	Cannavaro
5)	CON	3)	Halftime
6)	Laces	4)	Flag
8)	AR	7)	Shield
10)	Attacking	11)	Cover
13)	Arm	12)	My
14)	Volley	15)	Elbow
16)	Book	16)	Ball
18)	All	17)	Kaka
20)	Drop	19)	Leg
21)	Los Angeles		

Bonus: David Beckham.

p. 46: The Fung a Wing Puzzle

Cilly Foreshore, Fastah Slurpah, Cheesy Pops and Stern Westminstersunningson are fake.

p. 47: Scrambled Countries

1) Brazil
2) Argentina
3) Portugal
4) Japan
5) Denmark
6) England
7) Germany
8) Mexico
9) Italy
10) France
11) USA
12) Canada
13) Spain

The leftover letters spell out Czech Republic when unscrambled.

Bonus: 2006: Marta; 2005: Birgit Prinz; 2004: Birgit Prinz; 2003: Birgit Prinz; 2002: Mia Hamm; 2001: Mia Hamm.

p. 48: Sudo Soccer #2

	1	2	3	4	5	6	7	8	9
A	7	4	2	8	1	5	6	3	9
B	9	3	1	6	4	7	8	2	5
C	5	8	6	2	3	9	7	4	1
D	8	5	7	4	9	2	3	1	6
E	2	9	3	1	8	6	4	5	7
F	1	6	4	7	5	3	2	9	8
G	3	1	8	5	7	4	9	6	2
H	4	2	5	9	6	8	1	7	3
I	6	7	9	3	2	1	5	8	4

Bonus: Marta (February 1986), Cristiano Ronaldo (February 1985), Ronaldinho (March 1980), Ronaldo (September 1976), David Beckham (May 1975), Mia Hamm (March 1972).

p. 50: More Choice

1) D
2) B
3) A
4) B (May Day Stadium, built in 1989, is the world's largest non-racing stadium)
5) A
6) B
7) A
8) B
9) D
10) A

p. 52: What Am I? #2

A) Penalty Kick
B) Shinpads/Shinguards
C) Offside

p. 53: More Hidden Countries

The countries are: Cameroon, Canada, Chile, China, Colombia, Congo, Costa Rica, Croatia, Cuba and the Czech Republic.

Bonus: Chicago Fire, Chivas USA, Colorado Rapids, Columbus Crew, DC United, FC Dallas, Houston Dynamo, Kansas City Wizards, Los Angeles Galaxy, New England Revolution, Real Salt Lake, Red Bull New York, Toronto FC.

p. 54: Lost Ladies

H	G	Z	N	I	R	P	S	**B**	M
I	A	N	**R**	**G**	E	D	R	S	U
B	**I**	M	A	F	P	Y	E	I	R
N	E	**T**	M	L	O	O	K	**N**	R
I	L	N	**P**	E	O	L	A	C	A
A	I	G	G	E	H	L	T	L	Y
T	L	L	R	T	L	**R**	R	A	N
S	L	R	I	I	S	E	A	I	O
A	Y	M	M	N	N	S	M	R	H
H	S	C	E	G	G	O	**I**	C	
C	A	W	A	S	**N**	O	S	N	I
M	E	D	A	L	E	N	R	**Z**	P

The leftover letters spell Birgit Prinz.

The U.S. women's team has won the **Algarve Cup** five times in 12 appearances. The Cup is one of the most prestigious tournaments in the women's soccer world. Norway has won it the second-most, with four titles in 14 appearances, as of 2007.